New Brunswick

SPEM REDUXIT

Megan Lappi

WEIGL EDUCATIONAL PUBLISHERS

Published by Weigl Educational Publishers Limited
6325 10 Street SE
Calgary, Alberta, Canada
T2H 2Z9
Web site: www.weigl.com

We acknowledge the financial support of the Government of Canada through the Book Publishing
Industry Development Program (BPIDP) for our publishing activities.

National Library of Canada Cataloguing in Publication Data
Lappi, Megan
  New Brunswick / Megan Lappi.
  (Canadian sites and symbols)
  Includes index.
  ISBN 1-55388-029-3
  1. Provincial emblems--New Brunswick--Juvenile literature.
2. Heraldry--New Brunswick--Juvenile literature. I. Title.
II. Series.
CR213.N4L36 2003   j929.6'09715'1   C2003-910536-9

Printed in the United States of America
1 2 3 4 5 6 7 8 9 0   07 06 05 04 03

Project Coordinator: Donald Wells
Design: Janine Vangool
Layout: Terry Paulhus
Copy Editor: Tina Schwartzenberger
Photo Researchers: Pamela Wilton
                   Barbara Hoffman

Photograph Credits
Every reasonable effort has been made to trace ownership and to obtain permission to reprint
copyright material. The publishers would be pleased to have any errors or omissions brought to
their attention so that they may be corrected in subsequent printings.

Cover: man with lobster (**MaXx Images**); **Barrett & MacKay:** pages 3B, 4, 5, 11, 14, 16, 18, 21B, 22,
23; **Corel Corporation:** pages 3T, 3M, 7T, 12, 13T, 13B; **Ray Joubert:** page 10; ©**Bill Morgenstern/
Earth Moods:** page 15B; **National Archives of Canada:** page 6 (C-008744); **Photocanada.com:**
pages 7B, 15T, 20; **Photos.com:** pages 9, 17T, 21T; **Potash Corporation of Saskatchewan:** page 17B;
Provincial Government of New Brunswick: pages 1, 8, 19.

Contents

Introduction

Canada is a large country. The ten Canadian provinces and three territories cover a vast amount of land. From one province or territory to another, the people, lifestyles, land, and animals are quite different. Each province and territory has its own **identity**. The provinces and territories use **symbols** to represent this identity. This book looks at the symbols that represent the province of New Brunswick.

New Brunswick is well-known for its bridges. There are sixty-four covered bridges still standing in New Brunswick.

The province of New Brunswick is located on Canada's East Coast, west of the other three Atlantic provinces—Newfoundland and Labrador, Nova Scotia, and Prince Edward Island. Many people think that fishing is the most important industry in New Brunswick, but New Brunswick's largest industry is forestry. Thick, green forests cover a large part of the province. Most of New Brunswick's symbols represent the province's forests.

Fredericton, the capital of New Brunswick, was named for King George III's second son, Frederick.

New Brunswick is the only province in Canada that has two official languages—English and French.

Hartland, New Brunswick, is the smallest incorporated town in Canada, with a population of about 902.

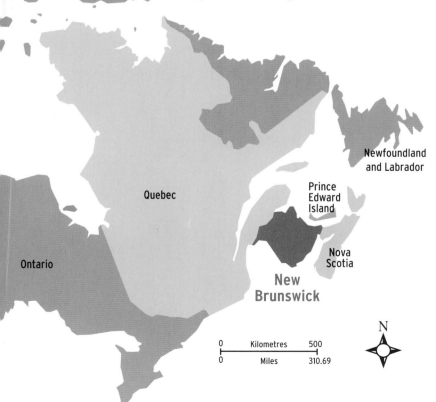

Ontario

Quebec

Newfoundland and Labrador

Prince Edward Island

Nova Scotia

New Brunswick

| 0 | Kilometres | 500 |
| 0 | Miles | 310.69 |

N

What's in a Name?

In 1784, the British king divided the colony of Nova Scotia into two parts. The new colony, New Brunswick, was named after the royal house of Brunswick-Lüneberg, the family of King George I of Great Britain. The original capital of New Brunswick was Saint John. It was difficult to defend Saint John against attack from the sea. The capital was moved inland to Fredericton. In the 1860s, New Brunswick was afraid that it might be attacked by the United States. To protect itself from attack, New Brunswick joined Confederation in 1867.

Saint John was known as a shipbuilding centre in the mid-1800s.

New Brunswick has often been referred to as the "Loyalist Province." It earned this nickname because many American colonists who were loyal to Great Britain during the American Revolution settled in New Brunswick. The Loyalists spoke English and settled in the southern parts of the province, mostly in cities. The French-speaking people of New Brunswick, also known as Acadians, settled in the northern and eastern parts of the province where they could farm and fish.

More than 62,000 square kilometres (23,938 square miles) of New Brunswick is covered by forests. This is about 85 percent of the province's total area.

With 730,000 people, New Brunswick is Canada's third-smallest province.

Saint John, settled in 1783, was the first city in Canada.

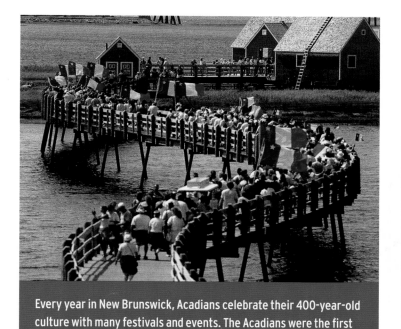

Every year in New Brunswick, Acadians celebrate their 400-year-old culture with many festivals and events. The Acadians were the first Europeans to settle in New Brunswick.

Coat of Arms Closeup

A coat of arms is a special design that represents a group or region. Every Canadian province and territory has its own coat of arms. New Brunswick's coat of arms links the province to its past. Each part of the design has a symbol that represents a different part of New Brunswick's **heritage**.

Fun Facts

Queen Victoria approved the original coat of arms in 1868.

Fiddleheads are a New Brunswick delicacy. These ferns are boiled and served with lemon and butter.

A fleur-de-lis is a **stylized** lily. In French, *fleur* means "flower," and *lis* means "lily."

SPEM REDUXIT

Features

The gold lion connects the province to the royal family of Brunswick-Lüneberg, for which it was named.

A ship with moving oars represents the province's shipping past.

The blue wavy lines below the ship link the province to the sea.

Two white-tailed deer on either side of the shield have crests hanging from their collars. One crest is the Union Jack, a symbol of Great Britain. The other crest is the fleur-de-lis, a symbol of France.

Fiddleheads, leaves of the ostrich fern, are growing below the deer's feet.

White-tailed deer

Beside the fiddleheads are purple violets, New Brunswick's provincial flower.

The Latin phrase *Spem Reduxit* at the bottom of the coat of arms means "Hope was restored."

Flying the Flag

In the early 1960s, New Brunswick did not have a provincial flag. In 1965, the premier of the province, Louis Joseph Robichaud, went on a vacation and left his administrative assistant, Robert Pichette, in charge. Pichette heard that the opposition party secretly planned to introduce an official flag for the province.

Even though the premier was away, Pichette needed to act quickly. He called his friend, artist Alan J. Beddoes, and together they came up with a design for the flag using two important symbols from the coat of arms. When the premier returned from his vacation, the government introduced the flag.

New Brunswick's flag became official in 1965. It has a golden lion on a red background and a ship sailing across the sea. The lion represents New Brunswick's connection to Great Britain. The ship represents New Brunswick's close relationship with the sea.

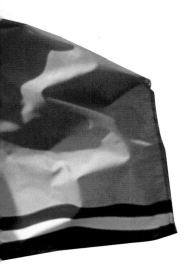

New Brunswick's Legislative Assembly building is known as the People's House. It was built in 1882.

Flying Squirrels and Chickadees

New Brunswick is home to many different animals. Some animals fly through the air, some swim through the water, and many more live deep in the province's forests. The larger animals in the forests include black bears, moose, white-tailed deer, and wildcats, such as lynx. There are also smaller animals, such as flying squirrels, martens, minks, muskrats, rabbits, and skunks.

Flying squirrels use flaps of skin between their legs to glide through the air as they jump from tree to tree. They almost never land on the ground.

New Brunswick's official bird is the black-capped chickadee, one of the most common birds in province. Its **distinctive** song, "chicka-dee-dee-dee," can be heard all year.

Other birds, such as the Atlantic puffin, are very unusual. The Atlantic puffin nests on rocky islands off the coast of New Brunswick in the Bay of Fundy. Unfortunately, because of **overfishing**, there are fewer fish off the Atlantic Coast, and the Atlantic puffin's young are threatened by this lack of food.

Every year the chickadee announces the arrival of spring by singing "chicka-dee-dee-dee." Chickadees hide food in secret locations in case they ever have trouble finding food.

Fun Facts

More than fifteen different whale species live off the coast of New Brunswick.

The Bay of Fundy has the world's highest tides. These tides can reach 14 metres (48 feet).

New Brunswick's Miramichi River is world famous for its salmon fishing.

Atlantic Forests

New Brunswick is one of the most **densely** forested areas in the world. Its forests are made up of different types of trees. New Brunswick's northern forests contain **coniferous** trees such as fir, spruce, and tamarack. In other parts of the province, there are mixed forests with birch, hemlock, and sugar maple trees.

The purple violet blooms every year from May to July. It became New Brunswick's provincial flower in 1936. Jam and syrup are made from the purple violet's flowers. Some people use the flowers as medicine for colds and coughs.

The purple violet is a very popular flower. Not only is it the provincial flower of New Brunswick, it is also the official state flower of Illinois, New Jersey, and Rhode Island.

The official tree of New Brunswick is the balsam fir. It has narrow, flat needles that are dark green on top and white underneath. The balsam fir is a **hardy** tree that can grow almost anywhere in the province and sometimes grows 20 metres (66 feet) high. The balsam fir is very important to New Brunswick's pulp and paper industry.

Balsam fir wood is one of the best woods for making paper because it is light, soft, and made of very long wood fibres. About 97 percent of New Brunswick's Christmas trees are balsam fir.

Fun Facts

New Brunswick is a producer of maple syrup. There are more than 12,000 maple syrup producers in Canada.

The town of Nackawic has the world's largest axe on display. It is 18 metres (60 feet) high.

On May 17, 1987, New Brunswick became the third province to adopt an official tree.

Emblems of the Earth

New Brunswick is known for its **lush** plant life. Blueberries and cranberries grow in the southwest. On the northeast coast, there are peat bogs in swampy areas. Peat is made of dead plants that have been **compressed**. It is sometimes cut up, dried, and burned as fuel.

New Brunswick does not have an official gem, mineral, or stone. Still, many people work in the mining industry, and mining is very important to New Brunswick's economy. New Brunswick's mining industry produces coal, copper, gold, lead, potash, silver, and zinc.

Berries are an important crop in New Brunswick. The strawberry industry in New Brunswick was worth $2 million in 2002.

New Brunswick has a zinc mine that produces the largest amount of zinc in the world. This mine was discovered by a geology student. The mine has produced $20 billion worth of minerals since it started operating in the 1950s. Many places in New Brunswick reflect the province's mining history, such as Grindstone Island, Lower Salt Springs, Plaster Rock, and Quarryville.

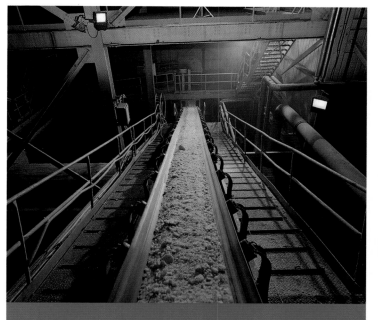

Potash is mined deep underground and then brought to the surface by a system of conveyor belts. Half of the world's potash comes from New Brunswick.

Fun Facts

The potato is New Brunswick's main crop.

Potash and salt were discovered in New Brunswick during the early 1970s.

Dulse is a tasty seaweed that grows in the water off the coast of New Brunswick.

The first ice cream cone was invented by Walter Donelly, a baker who lived in New Brunswick.

A Symbolic Tartan

New Brunswick has an official tartan. Tartans were first used by Scottish highlanders to represent their **clans**. The New Brunswick tartan is registered at the Court of the Lord Lyon, King of Arms in Scotland. It was designed in New Brunswick and became the official tartan in 1959.

New Brunswick celebrates its Scottish heritage with festivals that feature traditional music, clothing, and dances, such as the Highland Fling.

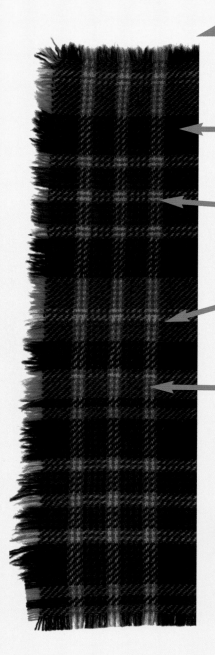

Features

New Brunswick's official tartan is made up of five colours that represent the province's landscape, early history, and bright future.

Dark green stands for New Brunswick's forests and its lumber industry.

Meadow green represents the thousands of farms in the province.

Blue is a reminder of the ocean that borders the province on two sides, as well as New Brunswick's lakes and rivers.

Red connects the tartan to the early Loyalist settlers who were loyal to Great Britain.

Gold is interwoven throughout the tartan as a symbol of New Brunswick's wealth of resources.

Fun Facts

New Brunswick's first Tartan Day was celebrated on April 6, 1993. Tartan Day honours the Scottish pioneers who settled in New Brunswick in 1621 and their descendants.

Special Places

Every province and territory has at least one special place that represents either its cultural or natural heritage. It could be a historic building, a monument, or a park. New Brunswick has several provincial parks and two national parks—Kouchibouguac (pronounced KOOSH-e-boo-gwac) National Park and Fundy National Park. Kouchibouguac National Park was established in 1969 in order to preserve the last of the lowlands in the maritime region. Fundy National Park was established in 1948 to preserve the coastline of the Bay of Fundy with its world-famous giant tides and Acadian forest.

There are ten nature trails through Kouchibouguac National Park. A single trail will pass through many different habitats, including freshwater, lagoon, forest, sand dunes, and fields.

Kouchibouguac National Park has many kilometres of wooden boardwalks that were built so people could walk across the salt **marshes** and sand dunes without damaging them. Fundy National Park is a coastal park that is known for its tidal flats, which are flat, barren areas of mud that are repeatedly covered by tides.

Another famous park is Rocks Provincial Park, located on the Bay of Fundy. Ninety-one billion tonnes (100 billion tons) of salt water move in and out of the Bay of Fundy every day.

In Rocks Provincial Park, the famous Fundy tide has carved the sandstone cliffs into tall, reddish rocks that have been nicknamed "flowerpots."

Fun Facts

Peregrine falcons disappeared from Fundy National Park but were successfully brought back to the park in 1982.

Kouchibouguac is a Mi'kmaq word that means "river of long tides."

The water that flows into the Bay of Fundy every 12.5 hours is nearly equal to the 24-hour flow of all the rivers in the world.

Quiz

Based on what you have read, see if you can answer the following questions:

1. What is the capital of New Brunswick?

2. What animal appears on New Brunswick's coat of arms?

3. Where does the word *Kouchibouguac* come from?

4. What kind of tree do most New Brunswickers decorate at Christmas?

The Hartland Covered Bridge, which spans the St. John River, is the longest covered bridge in the world. It is 391 metres (1,282 feet) long.

5. How much of New Brunswick is covered by forest?

6. How many different colours are on New Brunswick's tartan?

7. What is New Brunswick's official flower?

8. What is New Brunswick's top industry?

Employees at King's Landing Historical Settlement dress in period costumes and demonstrate traditional methods of framing and cooking.

Answers

8. Forestry

7. The purple violet

6. There are five colours on the tartan.

5. About 85 percent

4. The balsam fir

3. It is a Mi'kmaq word for "river of long tides."

2. The white-tailed deer

1. Fredericton

Glossary

clans: groups of people who are all related

compressed: pressed tightly together

coniferous: trees that have cones and needles

densely: crowded together

distinctive: something that is unusual

hardy: able to grow in all types of weather

heritage: something handed down from earlier generations

identity: the qualities that make one person or thing different from all others

lush: abundant green vegetation

marshes: land that is flooded with water

overfishing: when too many fish are taken by fishers

stylized: a style in which there are only a few simple details

symbols: things that stand for something else

Index